THE ULTIMATE
MANCHESTER UNITED
TRIVIA BOOK

A Collection of Amazing Trivia Quizzes
and Fun Facts for Die-Hard Man United Fans!

Ray Walker

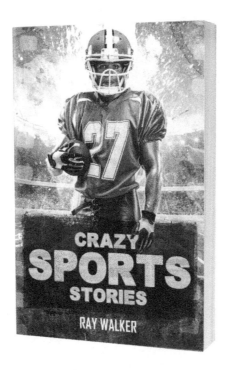

CONTENTS

INTRODUCTION

Manchester United is one of the most famous and richest football clubs in the history of the game. From the team's origins in the late 1800s as Newton Heath LYR Football Club to the conclusion of the 2019-2020 season, the club has been one of the most consistent both at home in England as well as in Europe and anywhere else it's played in the world.

Known across the globe as "the Red Devils," Man United currently holds the English record for most top-flight league championships in domestic play and has been crowned the champions of Europe on three occasions. The squad has also won dozens of other domestic and European trophies throughout its long, legendary history.

Many of the world's top players have suited up for the club and displayed their talents at famous grounds such as North Road, Bank Street, and Old Trafford.

Some of the best ever to grace these hallowed pitches include Duncan Edwards, George Best, Denis Law, Sir Bobby Charlton, Ryan Giggs, Paul Scholes, Patrice Evra, Eric Cantona, Wayne Rooney, Andy Cole, David Beckham, and Zlatan Ibrahimović, along with goalkeepers Alex Stepney, Peter Schmeichel, Edwin van der Sar, and David de Gea.

1

Even some of the club's managers have been as famous as the players, such as Sir Matt Busby, Sir Alex Ferguson, and José Mourinho.

Not everything has been rosy for the club, however, as the 1958 Munich air disaster claimed the lives of several of the young "Busby Babes" players, as well as others who were heading home aboard that fateful flight following a European Cup tie in the former nation of Yugoslavia.

There's absolutely no question that Manchester United has one of the most loyal and passionate fan bases in the world of sports. They have supported the club through the league titles and cup wins as well as the turbulent and controversial times.

This Manchester United trivia/fact book contains an abundance of facts about the club's history from the very humble beginnings right up to the conclusion of the 2019-20 campaign.

It offers a dozen chapters, each of which contains a quiz that challenges you with a combination of 20 multiple-choice and true-false brain puzzlers. The correct answers are revealed on another page. Every chapter also features 10 historical "Did You Know?" facts about Man United's history, players, managers, etc.

Man United supporters can quickly sharpen their quiz-taking skills with the book as they refresh and relive many of the team's most famous and historic moments. In fact, you may even be able to pick up some new information on the team along the way. It's an ideal way to prepare yourself for quiz and trivia challenges from family members and fellow fans.

Hopefully, you'll enjoy this historic trip back in time and realize why you're such a passionate fan of mighty Manchester United.

CHAPTER 1:

ORIGINS & HISTORY

QUIZ TIME!

1. What year was the club founded?

    a. 1879

    b. 1882

    c. 1878

    d. 1880

2. The club was a founding member of which league in 1888?

    a. Football Alliance

    b. The Combination

    c. The Football League

    d. The Lancashire Railway Workers League

3. Before being named Manchester United, the team was known as Newton Heath LYR Football Club.

    a. True

    b. False

4. Who became the club's president in 1902?

    a. Frederick Attock

    b. Ernest Mangnall

    c. John Henry Davies

    d. John James Bentley

5. How many wins did the squad record in its first season in the Football League in 1892-93?

    a. 5

    b. 7

    c. 4

    d. 6

6. When did Man United win its first league title?

    a. 1906

    b. 1907

    c. 1908

    d. 1909

7. Against which team did the club play its first recorded game on November 20, 1880?

    a. Old Etonians Association FC

    b. Clapham Rovers

    c. Nottingham Forrest

    d. Bolton Wanderers Reserves

8. The club played its first competitive match against Blackburn Olympic Reserves in 1883.

    a. True

    b. False

9. Where did Man United play its home games from 1880 to 1893?

    a. Bank Street
    b. North Road
    c. Dudley Road
    d. Pike's Lane

10. Man United was integral to forming the league's players union and was given which nickname in the process?

    a. The Strikers
    b. Manchester Union
    c. Players United
    d. The Outcasts

11. After joining the Football League, Newton Heath spent two seasons in the First Division before being relegated.

    a. True
    b. False

12. How many goals did the outfit score in its first season in the Football League First Division?

    a. 30
    b. 44
    c. 50
    d. 52

13. How many times has the club been relegated as of 2020?

    a. 5
    b. 3
    c. 6
    d. 4

14. The team's debut as Manchester United occurred in the Football League's First Division.

    a. True
    b. False

15. Which team did Man United face in its first Test Match to avoid relegation in 1892-93?

    a. Small Heath
    b. Darwen
    c. Sheffield United
    d. Grimsby Town

16. Which of the club's financial supporters funded its move to Old Trafford?

    a. John Chapman
    b. John Robson
    c. John Henry Davies
    d. James W. Gibson

17. What was the final score of Newton Heath's first match and victory in the Combination League against Darwen in September 1888?

    a. 2-1
    b. 1-0
    c. 4-3
    d. 4-1

18. What year did the club officially re-brand itself as Manchester United?

    a. 1903
    b. 1902

c. 1900

d. 1905

19. Which team did Manchester United face in its inaugural match at Old Trafford in February 1910?

a. Sunderland

b. Newcastle United

c. Chelsea

d. Liverpool

20. When the Football Alliance and Football League merged in 1892-93, Newton Heath was placed in the First Division.

a. True

b. False

QUIZ ANSWERS

1. C – 1878

2. B – The Combination

3. A – True

4. C – John Henry Davies

5. D – 6

6. C – 1908

7. D – Bolton Wanderers Reserves

8. A – True

9. B – North Road

10. D – The Outcasts

11. A – True

12. C – 50

13. A – 5

14. B – False

15. A – Small Heath

16. C – John Henry Davies

17. C – 4-3

18. B – 1902

19. D – Liverpool

20. A – True

DID YOU KNOW?

1. Manchester United of the English Premier League was originally founded in 1878 in the city of Manchester, Lancashire, England, as Newton Heath LYR Football Club. LYR was the Lancashire and Yorkshire Railway Company, where the club's players were employed. The team, based in the carriage and wagon department, played against other departments and railway companies. They competed in their first recorded contest in November 1880, losing 6-0 to Bolton Wanderers' reserve squad.

2. The club was a founding member of a regional league known as The Combination in 1888. The league disbanded after a year, and Newton Heath then joined the newly created Football Alliance for three seasons before the Alliance merged with the Football League. The club competed in the First Division in 1892-93 and was simply known as Newton Heath, as LYR was dropped from the name.

3. The club's first home ground was North Road from 1878 to 1893, then Bank Street from 1893 to 1910, and finally Old Trafford from 1910 to the present. Another Manchester-based team known as Manchester Football Club was founded in 1860 and later became a rugby club.

4. After a new group of local businessmen took over, Newton Heath was re-branded as Manchester United in

1902. The team is now nicknamed "the Red Devils." They are also known simply as "United," "Man United," "Man Utd," or "Man U" by some fans. The team won its first Division 1 league title in 1907-08 and captured its first English FA Cup in 1908-09.

5. Man United is currently owned by Manchester United PLC and is listed on the London Stock Exchange and the New York Stock Exchange. The Glazer family of America has been the majority owners of the franchise since 2005. They also own the Tampa Bay Buccaneers of the National Football League (NFL) in America.

6. The North Road ground where Newton Heath was located was close to the railway company and had a capacity of approximately 12,000. However, club officials believed the venue was inadequate for a team that aspired to join the Football League. The stadium was expanded in 1887 and 1891, as a pair of grandstands was added. The highest recorded attendance at North Road was 15,000 for a game against Sunderland in March 1893.

7. The club was sent packing from North Road by the ground's owners because Newton Heath charged admission for its contests. In June 1893, they started to use the Bank Street ground in nearby Clayton, and two stands were built to accommodate thousands of more fans. Newton Heath's first league outing at Bank Street attracted 10,000 fans, who witnessed Alf Farman notch all three goals in a 3-2 victory over Burnley on September 1, 1893.

8. Old Trafford was announced as the new home of Manchester United in February 1909, when the land was bought for approximately £60,000. The stadium, which is nicknamed "The Theatre of Dreams," was originally supposed to hold 100,000 people, but this was revised to 77,000 due to costs. The earliest record attendance was recorded in March 1939, when 76,962 showed up for an FA Cup semifinal between Grimsby Town and Wolverhampton Wanderers.

9. Old Trafford suffered serious bombing damage in World War II. While it was being rebuilt, the team played its home games at Maine Road, the home of crosstown rivals Manchester City. Man United paid a fee of £5,000 plus a small percentage of gate receipts per year to use Maine Road. All-seating rules reduced fan capacity to 44,000 in 1993. Further redevelopment enabled the stadium to host 76,098 fans in March 2007, when Man United beat the Blackburn Rovers 4-1. The current capacity is listed as 75,957.

10. Manchester United became the first English club, and second from Britain, to capture the European Cup when they beat Benfica of Portugal 4-1 in 1968. The game, which drew a crowd of 92,225 to Wembley Stadium in London, was tied 1-1 after 90 minutes. Man United then scored three goals in a span of seven minutes in extra time for the triumph.

CHAPTER 2:

THE CAPTAIN CLASS

QUIZ TIME!

1. Who was the first player recorded as captain of Newton Heath from 1882-83?

    a. E. Thomas
    b. Bob McFarlane
    c. Sam Black
    d. Jack Powell

2. Who was the first captain of Manchester United in 1902-03?

    a. Charlie Roberts
    b. Jack Peddie
    c. James McNaught
    d. Harry Stafford

3. As of 2020, there have been 60 players appointed as full-time captain of Man United and Newton Heath combined.

    a. True
    b. False

4. For how many matches did Joe Cassidy serve as captain of Newton Heath?

    a. 99
    b. 146
    c. 170
    d. 163

5. Which player served as Man United's skipper for the most years?

    a. Bryan Robson
    b. Wayne Rooney
    c. Martin Buchan
    d. Bobby Charlton

6. Who served as captain from 1973 to 1975?

    a. Sammy McIlroy
    b. Alex Stepney
    c. Willie Morgan
    d. George Graham

7. How many full-time captains have Man United had in the Premier League era as of 2020?

    a. 9
    b. 10
    c. 11
    d. 12

8. Jack Powell captained Newton Heath in its first-ever competitive match.

    a. True
    b. False

9. How many captains did the club have between 2000 and 2010?

    a. 1
    b. 2
    c. 3
    d. 4

10. As of 2020, how many full-time captains have been midfielders/half backs?

    a. 20
    b. 18
    c. 13
    d. 16

11. In January 2020, Man United named Phil Jones captain of the club.

    a. True
    b. False

12. Which former captain was NOT a defender?

    a. Antonio Valencia
    b. Nemanja Vidić
    c. Gary Neville
    d. Denis Law

13. Which captain has won the most trophies with Man United as of 2020?

    a. Gary Neville
    b. Martin Buchan
    c. Roy Keane
    d. Wayne Rooney

14. Wayne Rooney was the last forward to captain the club as of 2020.

    a. True
    b. False

15. Who was skipper in 1914-15?

    a. Frank Barson
    b. Patrick O'Connell
    c. Jack Wilson
    d. George Hunter

16. Who was the first captain of the club NOT born in the British Isles?

    a. Robin van Persie
    b. Antonio Valencia
    c. Nemanja Vidić
    d. Eric Cantona

17. Louis Page was full-time captain for the fewest games in club history at how many?

    a. 36
    b. 14
    c. 23
    d. 12

18. Who was Man United's first non-British full-time captain?

    a. Bill McKay
    b. Stan Pearson
    c. John Carey
    d. Noel Cantwell

19. Who captained the club for 606 domestic league matches?

a. Bobby Charlton

b. Gary Neville

c. William Anthony Foulkes

d. Bryan Robson

20. There have been just five forwards acting as full-time captain as of 2020.

a. True

b. False

QUIZ ANSWERS

1. A – E. Thomas

2. D – Harry Stafford

3. B – False

4. D – 163

5. A – Bryan Robson

6. C – Willie Morgan

7. C – 11

8. A – True

9. B – 2

10. B – 18

11. B – False

12. D – Denis Law

13. C – Roy Keane

14. A – True

15. B – Patrick O'Connell

16. D – Eric Cantona

17. D – 12

18. C – John Carey

19. A – Bobby Charlton

20. B – False

DID YOU KNOW?

1. Man United has had a total of 50 known full-time captains since the club was formed as Newton Heath LYR F.C. in 1878. The current skipper as of September 2020 is defender Harry Maguire, who has also captained England's national team on several occasions. Maguire moved to Man United from Leicester City in 2019 for a reported £80 million, setting a world transfer record for a defender. However, his captaincy may be in jeopardy after he ran afoul of the law in Greece during the summer of 2020.

2. The first recorded captain of Newton Heath was simply known as E. Thomas, who held the position in 1882 and 1883. He was followed by Sam Black, Jack Powell, Bob McFarlane, and Joe Cassidy. However, the skipper for 1893-94 was unknown. There was no competitive football played from 1940 to 1944 due to World War II.

3. A total of 30 full-time captains were English, 11 were Scottish, four came from the Republic of Ireland, and two hailed from Wales. One each came from France, Ecuador, and Serbia. Jack Silcock was captain in 1930-31 and again from 1932 to 1934, while Bill McKay held the title from 1934-35 and again from 1939-40. George Roughton was skipper from 1937 to 1939 and again in 1944-45.

4. The first non-British skipper was Johnny Carey of the Republic of Ireland. Eric Cantona of France was the first

captain from outside of the British Isles (Scotland, England, Wales, Northern Ireland, and the Republic of Ireland). The first and only non-European full-time captain as of 2020 was Antonio Valencia of Ecuador. Noel Cantwell of the Republic of Ireland and Denis Law of Scotland were co-captains between 1964 and 1967.

5. Harry Stafford was the squad's skipper in 1897, when the club was Newton Heath, and held the job until 1903, when the club officially changed its name to Manchester United. Stafford had formerly played for Crewe Alexandra and made his Newton Heath debut in 1896 as a right-back. He was a driving force in getting J.H. Davies to help bail the club out when it was in financial difficulty in 1902.

6. Midfielder Bryan Robson was the side's longest-serving captain, as he held the position from 1982 to 1994. However, he shared the duties with defender Steve Bruce during the last two years of his stint. Robson appeared in 461 games with Man United and logged 99 goals. He also captained the English national team 65 times in his 90 outings.

7. Irish international Roy Keane wore the captain's armband from 1997 to 2005 and won the most trophies while holding the job. Keane helped the club capture four Premier League titles, two FA Cups, a Community Shield Trophy, a UEFA Champions League title, and one Intercontinental Cup. Keane played in 480 matches with the team and also captained the Republic of Ireland squad on numerous occasions in his 67 appearances.

8. Antonio Valencia of Ecuador played right-back and right wing after signing for Man United in June 2009. He was voted to the PFA Team of the Year in his first campaign with the team and went on to help the side win two Premier League crowns, an FA Cup, two League Cups, three FA Community Shields, and the UEFA Europa League. Valencia then returned to his homeland in 2019 to sign with LDU Quito.

9. John Joseph Carey of Dublin, Ireland, was known as Johnny Carey and Jackie Carey and was skipper of Man United from 1945 until 1953. Carey was a dual internationalist who played for both Irish international teams and also captained them. He was voted the Football Writers' Association Footballer of the Year in 1949 and became the first non-British player and first Irishman to skipper a title-winning side in the First Division and FA Cup final. Carey played nine different positions during his career, even once appearing in goal for Man United.

10. One of the longest-serving captains was Scottish international defender Martin Buchan as he held the title from 1975 to 1983. When he signed for Man United from Scottish club Aberdeen in 1972 for £120,000, he was the side's record signing at the time. When Man United beat Liverpool in the 1977 FA Cup Final, Buchan became the first player to captain an English and Scottish FA Cup winner as he also led Aberdeen to a Cup. He left in 1983 after playing 456 games with Man United.

CHAPTER 3:

AMAZING MANAGERS

QUIZ TIME!

1. As of 2020, how many known managers/secretaries/caretakers has the club had?

    a. 24

    b. 18

    c. 22

    d. 20

2. Whom did the club name as caretaker-manager on December 19, 2018?

    a. Bryan Barry-Murphy

    b. Carlos Corberán

    c. Ole Gunnar Solskjær

    d. Sam Ricketts

3. When the club first started operating as Newton Heath, there were four acting managers.

    a. True

    b. False

4. How many losses did Man United suffer under manager Sir Matt Busby?

    a. 307
    b. 285
    c. 300
    d. 292

5. Who was Man United's first player-manager?

    a. Lal Hilditch
    b. Ryan Giggs
    c. Herbert Bamlett
    d. Rio Ferdinand

6. Who was the first manager of Newton Heath from 1892 to 1900?

    a. James West
    b. John Bentley
    c. Jack Robson
    d. A.H. Albut

7. How many draws did manager Tommy Docherty record in his 228 matches with the club?

    a. 56
    b. 47
    c. 58
    d. 62

8. Ernest Mangnall was the first manager in the club's history to win a title.

    a. True
    b. False

9. How many goals did the club score under manager Ron Atkinson?

    a. 470

    b. 290

    c. 333

    d. 461

10. Which manager has won the most titles/trophies in club history?

    a. Ernest Mangnall

    b. Matt Busby

    c. José Mourinho

    d. Alex Ferguson

11. José Mourinho had more losses and draws combined than wins while managing the club.

    a. True

    b. False

12. How many matches did Ryan Giggs serve as temporary manager?

    a. 6

    b. 12

    c. 4

    d. 15

13. Which manager's squads conceded 1,536 goals?

    a. Herbert Bamlett

    b. Matt Busby

    c. Alex Ferguson

    d. Scott Duncan

14. Between June 4, 1969, and December 19, 1972, Man United had three different managers.

    a. True
    b. False

15. Dave Sexton won how many games as manager of the club?

    a. 84
    b. 57
    c. 92
    d. 81

16. How many matches did Alex Ferguson serve as Man United's manager?

    a. 1,470
    b. 1,500
    c. 1,120
    d. 1,250

17. Who was NOT one of the club's three managers between June 4, 1969, and December 19, 1972?

    a. Wilf McGuinness
    b. Frank O'Farrell
    c. Jimmy Murphy
    d. Matt Busby

18. How many managers have won more than 50 matches as of 2020?

    a. 7
    b. 10

c. 11

d. 9

19. Who managed the club when they became Manchester United?

   a. John Chapman

   b. James West

   c. John Bentley

   d. Ernest Mangnall

20. Ole Gunnar Solskjær won his first seven games as the club's caretaker before being hired as the full-time manager.

   a. True

   b. False

QUIZ ANSWERS

1. A – 24

2. C – Ole Gunnar Solskjær

3. B – False

4. D – 292

5. A – Lal Hilditch

6. D – A.H. Albut

7. C – 58

8. A – True

9. D – 461

10. D – Alex Ferguson

11. B – False

12. C – 4

13. B – Matt Busby

14. A – True

15. D – 81

16. B – 1,500

17. C – Jimmy Murphy

18. C – 11

19. B – James West

20. A – True

DID YOU KNOW?

1. It's unknown exactly who was in charge of the club between 1878 and 1892 because the team was selected by a committee. Those known to take care of the manager's duties were A.H. Albut in 1892; he was followed in succession by James West, T.J. Wallworth, Ernest Mangnall, and John Bentley.

2. The first of the club's known managers was considered to be Jack Robson in December 1914. He was followed by John Chapman, Lal Hilditch, Herbert Bamlett, Walter Crickmer, Scott Duncan, Walter Crickmer again, Matt Busby, Jimmy Murphy, Wilf McGuinness, Matt Busby again, Frank O'Farrell, Tommy Docherty, Dave Sexton, Ron Atkinson, Alex Ferguson, David Moyes, Ryan Giggs, Louis van Gaal, José Mourinho, and Ole Gunnar Solskjær.

3. Clarence "Lal" Hilditch was listed as a player-manager for 1926-27 and Jimmy Murphy as caretaker-manager in 1958. In addition, Ryan Giggs was an interim player-manager in 2014. Of the 19 managers, seven were English, six were Scottish, two were Welsh, and one each hailed from Portugal, Holland, the Republic of Ireland, and Norway.

4. The longest-serving and most successful manager of Man United has been Sir Alex Ferguson of Scotland. "Fergie" won 13 Premier League titles, 10 Community Shields, five FA Cups, four League Cups, two UEFA Champions

League titles, one UEFA Cup Winners' Cup, one UEFA Super Cup, one Intercontinental Cup, and one FIFA Club World Cup. Ferguson held the job from November 6, 1986, to May 19, 2013, and was in charge for 1,500 games.

5. Sir Alex Ferguson feuded with several managers, including former Liverpool boss Rafael Benitez, once saying that Benitez's defensive tactics were ruining the game and that Liverpool was unimaginative. Ferguson later wrote in his autobiography that Benitez turned it into a personal rather than football-related rivalry. Benitez went on a famous rant in 2009 when he presented "facts" to back up his criticism of Ferguson. When Benitez was asked about Ferguson's book, he claimed he had nothing to say as Ferguson didn't deserve the publicity.

6. Former Arsenal manager Arsène Wenger also feuded with Sir Alex Ferguson after Ferguson labeled him a novice when he arrived at Arsenal in 1996 from managing in Japan. Wenger was successful in England, but Ferguson always claimed his squad was better, even after Wenger's team went undefeated in 2003-04. Ferguson often belittled Wenger in the media, with Wenger refusing to shake hands after matches several times. The rivalry boiled over in 2004, when Man United halted Arsenal's 49-game unbeaten streak at Old Trafford. Ferguson was hit by a flying pizza in the tunnel after the match, and a brawl between the teams ensued.

7. Another volatile manager was José Mourinho, especially when it came to his nemesis, Pep Guardiola. The two

opposed each other often while managing in Spain, and the bad blood carried over when Mourinho was in charge of Man United and Guardiola was boss of Manchester City. In a December 2017 game at Old Trafford, a post-match brawl erupted when Mourinho allegedly stormed City's dressing room and was promptly drilled in the head with a water bottle.

8. José Mourinho won the League Cup, Community Shield, and UEFA Europa League in 2016-17 during his first campaign in charge but failed to win anything in 2017-18. He was then fired on December 18, 2018, after Man United won just seven of their first 17 games. Ole Gunnar Solskjær was then appointed as caretaker-manager for the rest of the season. In January 2019, he won his first seven matches in charge and was given the full-time job on March 28.

9. Sir Matt Busby was another legendary Man United manager, even though he played with enemies Liverpool and Manchester City. His young squads were nicknamed "The Busby Babes." The Scotsman managed the side from 1945 to 1969 and again for the final half of the 1970-71 campaign. He was the first to manage an English club to a European title, and he helped Man United capture 13 major trophies while with the club. Busby was in charge of the squad for a total of 1,141 contests.

10. Sir Matt Busby won the league title with the "Busby Babes" in 1955-56 and 1956-57 and reached the FA Cup Final twice. However, many players had their careers cut short in 1958 when the Munich air disaster took place, and

Busby was left fighting for his life. The team's plane crashed on February 6 when attempting to take off from a snow-covered runway in Munich where it stopped to refuel on the way home from Yugoslavia. A total of 23 of the 44 people aboard lost their lives. Assistant Jimmy Murphy took over as manager while Busby recovered in hospital.

CHAPTER 4:

DARING DEFENDERS

QUIZ TIME!

1. How many goals did Ashley Grimes score in his 107 games with the team?

   a. 3
   b. 4
   c. 5
   d. 11

2. Which defender scored 19 goals in 50 matches across all competitions in 1990-91?

   a. Clayton Blackmore
   b. Mal Donaghy
   c. Denis Irwin
   d. Steve Bruce

3. Defender Mike Duxbury was the first player to receive a red card in FA Cup Final history in 1985.

   a. True
   b. False

4. How many appearances did Denis Irwin make for Man United?

   a. 531

   b. 529

   c. 498

   d. 559

5. In which season did Nemanja Vidić join Man United?

   a. 2005-06

   b. 2006-07

   c. 2007-08

   d. 2008-09

6. Which defender scored only eight goals in 400 total appearances for the club?

   a. Jack Silcock

   b. Gary Pallister

   c. Rio Ferdinand

   d. Martin Buchan

7. Which player racked up 54 yellow cards in 397 league matches for Man United?

   a. Phil Neville

   b. Tony Dunne

   c. Gary Neville

   d. Ashley Young

8. Former Man United defender Wes Brown played most of his matches as a right-back.

   a. True

   b. False

9. Who scored the winning goal in the 1967-68 European Cup semifinal against Real Madrid?

    a. Francis Burns

    b. Nobby Stiles

    c. David Sadler

    d. Bill Foulkes

10. Who made 485 appearances across his 14-year career with the club?

    a. Brian McClair

    b. Tony Dunne

    c. Arthur Albiston

    d. Martin Buchan

11. Jaap Stam's only Man United goal came during the club's 1998-99 FA Cup run.

    a. True

    b. False

12. How many goals did Roger Byrne score in his 245 league appearances for Man United?

    a. 17

    b. 20

    c. 13

    d. 5

13. Which defender started 34 league matches in 2012-13?

    a. Chris Smalling

    b. Jonny Evans

    c. Patrice Evra

    d. Rafael

14. Gary Pallister was the first Man United defender to win the PFA Players' Player of the Year award.

    a. True

    b. False

15. Which defender earned four assists in the 2019-20 Premier League?

    a. Ashley Young

    b. Luke Shaw

    c. Aaron Wan-Bissaka

    d. Harry Maguire

16. How many defenders scored at least one goal in the 2006-07 domestic league?

    a. 7

    b. 6

    c. 3

    d. 4

17. Who won the UEFA Club Best Defender of the Year award in 1998-99?

    a. Henning Berg

    b. Nicky Butt

    c. Denis Irwin

    d. Jaap Stam

18. Which defender scored three goals and one assist in all competitions in 1998-99?

    a. Ronny Johnsen

    b. Wes Brown

c. John Curtis

d. Nicky Butt

19. Who received three red cards in the 2016-17 Europa League?

a. Antonio Valencia

b. Marcos Rojo

c. Eric Bailly

d. Daley Blind

20. Chris Smalling earned two red cards in the 2013-14 Premier League.

a. True

b. False

QUIZ ANSWERS

1. D – 11

2. D – Steve Bruce

3. B – False

4. B – 529

5. A – 2005-06

6. C – Rio Ferdinand

7. C – Gary Neville

8. B – False

9. D – Bill Foulkes

10. C – Arthur Albiston

11. B – False

12. A – 17

13. C – Patrice Evra

14. A – True

15. C – Aaron Wan-Bissaka

16. B – 6

17. D – Jaap Stam

18. A – Ronny Johnsen

19. C – Eric Bailly

20. B – False

DID YOU KNOW?

1. Phil Neville always seemed to be overshadowed by his older brother Gary, but the English international still enjoyed a fine career. Neville played 386 times with Man United from 1994 to 2005 before joining Everton. He also appeared in 59 matches with England and became a commentator with Sky Sports in the U.K. Neville returned to Man United in 2013 as first-team coach when David Moyes was hired as manager but was relieved when Louis van Gaal replaced Moyes in July 2014.

2. Like his brother Phil, Gary Neville also became a commentator with Sky Sports and dabbled in coaching and management. The former captain played his entire pro career with Man United from 1992 to 2011 and appeared 85 times internationally for England. He won 20 pieces of silverware with the club and chipped in with seven goals in 602 total appearances. Neville is a co-owner of the Salford City team with several ex-Man United teammates.

3. Serbian international Nemanja Vidić arrived from Spartak Moscow in January 2006 and made an instant impact, becoming one of the club's most valuable defenders. The former captain stayed with the team until 2014 when he joined Inter Milan. Vidić was strong in the air and took no prisoners on the ground due to his legendary toughness. He helped Man United capture five Premier League titles,

three League Cups, one FIFA Club World Cup, and a Champions League crown. He was named the Premier League Player of the Season twice, and he made the PFA Team of the Year four times.

4. French international defender Patrice Evra also joined Man United in January 2006 from Monaco and eventually skippered the side for several games. He went on to win five English Premier League titles with the team along with a Champions League crown, one FIFA Club World Cup, and three League Cups before he left for Juventus in 2014. He possessed excellent speed, reflexes, and crossing ability, even though he was just 5 feet 8 inches tall, and he was named to the PFA Team of the Year three times.

5. Most fans considered Spanish international Gerard Pique to be one of the best defenders in the world while playing with Barcelona. However, they may forget that the center-back got his feet wet as a professional footballer with Man United. Pique was basically a reserve while at Old Trafford, though, as he made only 23 total appearances between 2004 and 2008 and also spent time on loan with Zaragoza of Spain. He then hit the big time when arriving in Barcelona in 2008.

6. Defender David May was in the right place at the right time with Man United in 1998-99 after being acquired from Blackburn in 1994. The team won the Champions League, FA Cup, and Premier League title that season, and May left in 2003 with two Premier League and FA Cup winners medals. He appeared in just 85 league games and

contributed six goals. May was loaned several times and left for Burnley in 2003.

7. Tom Jones may be a famous singer, but Man United also had a Welshman by the same name in its squad. Jones, one of 14 children, was signed by the club from Oswestry Town and made his debut in November 1924. He helped the squad win promotion from the Second Division during his first campaign and went on to appear in more than 200 games in all competitions. His last league match for Man United came in the 1936-37 season.

8. Former English international Rio Ferdinand played 504 Premier League games with several teams; 312 of those league matches coming with Man United. He concentrated on defending and managed just 11 goals in his league outings, with 7 of them coming for United. Ferdinand was an England regular for the majority of his career and notched three goals in 81 senior contests. Rio is the brother of Anton and cousin of Kane and Les Ferdinand.

9. Dennis Irwin was a solid Man United and Irish international defender who played with the club between 1990 and 2002. Sir Alex Ferguson once said that, pound for pound, Irwin was his best-ever signing. He played 529 times for United and 56 times for the Republic of Ireland. Along with former Man United player Roy Keane, Irwin is the most successful Irish player in history as they each won 19 trophies in their careers.

10. In August 2020, Victor Lindelöf was a defender of the peace rather than on the pitch when the Swedish

international intervened to stop the robbery of a 90-year-old woman in his hometown of Vasteras. After a man riding a bicycle stole the woman's purse, Lindelöf ran after the thief and pinned him to the ground until police arrived to make an arrest. The defender received thank you's from both the victim and the police department with a spokesperson remarking, "The man who intervened very resourcefully was athletically built. Obviously, the person who caught the thief was good at short sprints."

CHAPTER 5:

GOALTENDING GREATS

QUIZ TIME!

1. How many clean sheets did Fabien Barthez have in 2000-01 domestic league matches?

    a. 17

    b. 14

    c. 12

    d. 9

2. Massimo Taibi allowed how many goals in his final game with Man United in a 1999 loss to Chelsea?

    a. 4

    b. 3

    c. 6

    d. 5

3. As of 2020, 91 keepers have appeared in at least one match for Man United.

    a. True

    b. False

4. Which goalie made only 35 saves in 1994-95 league matches?

   a. Gary Walsh
   b. Peter Schmeichel
   c. Kevin Pilkington
   d. Edwin van der Sar

5. Which keeper helped Man United win its first league title in 1907-08?

   a. Jack Mew
   b. Bobby Beale
   c. Harry Moger
   d. Frank Barrett

6. Who has made the most appearances in goal for the club as of 2020?

   a. Gary Bailey
   b. David de Gea
   c. Peter Schmeichel
   d. Alex Stepney

7. Which keeper was Edwin van der Sar's backup in 62 games from 2006-07 to 2010-11?

   a. Tomasz Kuszczak
   b. Ben Amos
   c. Anders Lindegaard
   d. Ben Foster

8. Star keeper Victor Valdés played just 12 matches with Man United.

a. True

b. False

9. How many matches did Alex Stepney play for Man United?

    a. 559

    b. 566

    c. 539

    d. 485

10. How many clean sheets did Peter Schmeichel record in league matches for Man United?

    a. 128

    b. 115

    c. 120

    d. 112

11. In 57 appearances in all competitions with the club, Sergio Romero has recorded 37 clean sheets.

    a. True

    b. False

12. Which player from Benfica did Alex Stepney make one of his most famous saves against to send the 1968 European Cup into extra time?

    a. Eusébio

    b. Georges Bereta

    c. José Augusto

    d. José Torres

13. Which keeper infamously conceded a goal through his legs to Matt Le Tissier in 1999?

    a. Mark Bosnich
    b. Nick Culkin
    c. Massimo Taibi
    d. Raimond van der Gouw

14. David de Gea currently owns the club record for 14 consecutive games with a clean sheet.

    a. True
    b. False

15. Which keeper conceded a penalty but redeemed himself by saving it in his 2003 debut?

    a. Fabien Barthez
    b. Tim Howard
    c. Ricardo
    d. Roy Carroll

16. How many total appearances did Tim Howard make with the team?

    a. 45
    b. 56
    c. 41
    d. 52

17. Which keeper played 64 matches with Newton Heath/Man United from 1900 to 1903?

    a. John Sutcliffe
    b. Herbert Birchenough

c. James Saunders

d. Jimmy Whitehouse

18. How many keepers have made at least one appearance for the club in the Premier League?

    a. 20

    b. 22

    c. 19

    d. 21

19. How many clean sheets did Roy Carroll keep in 46 league matches with Man United?

    a. 16

    b. 18

    c. 22

    d. 24

20. Edwin van der Sar was 34 years old when he joined Man United.

    a. True

    b. False

QUIZ ANSWERS

1. B – 14

2. D – 5

3. A – True

4. A – Gary Walsh

5. C – Harry Moger

6. D – Alex Stepney

7. A – Tomasz Kuszczak

8. B – False

9. C – 539

10. D – 112

11. A – True

12. A – Eusébio

13. C – Massimo Taibi

14. B – False

15. C – Ricardo

16. D – 52

17. D – Jimmy Whitehouse

18. B – 22

19. D – 24

20. A – True

DID YOU KNOW?

1. French international Fabien Barthez may have conceded a few howlers, but he was one of the most entertaining and best keepers around. He joined Man United in 2000 from Monaco after winning the 1998 World Cup with his homeland. He shares the World Cup record with England's Peter Shilton for most clean sheets in the event with 10. Barthez made 139 appearances with the team and helped them win the Premier League in 2001-02 and 2002-03 and was named to the 2000-01 PFA Team of the Year.

2. Italian goalkeeper Massimo Taibi was acquired in 1999 from Venezia but struggled with the club. He played a grand total of four league games with the squad and conceded some stoppable goals. This included five in a contest against Chelsea and an infamous howler against Southampton's Matthew Le Tissier. He was loaned back to the Italian Serie A soon after with Reggina in January 2000. To his credit, Taibi received man of the match honors in a 3-2 triumph over Liverpool even though he conceded another howler.

3. One of the greatest keepers the world has ever seen was Peter Schmeichel, whose play for Man United in 1995-96 was exceptional. The former Danish international helped the squad capture the FA Cup and Premier League title as United became the first English side to win the double

twice. Schmeichel was named to the Premier League Team of the Year as well as being named the league's Player of the Year. He earned 18 clean sheets in 36 league outings and 22 in all competitions. He also tallied a late equalizer in a 2-2 UEFA Cup contest against Rotor Volgograd.

4. Spanish international David de Gea joined Man United from Atletico Madrid in 2011. After initially struggling, he became one of the squad's most valuable players. As of 2020, he was named the team's Player of the Year a record three consecutive times from 2014 to 2016 and four times in total. He's made over 400 appearances, won a Premier League title, FA Cup, League Cup, and the UEFA Europa League. De Gea has also been named to five PFA Teams of the Year and was named to the FIFA FIFPro World XI in 2018.

5. Former Dutch international Edwin van der Sar played with Man United from 2005 to 2011 and helped capture Premier League honors in four of his six seasons. He also won a League Cup, UEFA Champions League title, and FIFA Club World Cup. He finished his Premier League career with 134 clean sheets in 313 matches, which placed him in a sixth-place tie at the time. Van der Sar posted 21 clean sheets one season, and in 2008-09, set a world league record by not allowing a goal for 1,311 minutes. He's also the oldest player to win the Premier League at 40 years and 205 days old.

6. Keeper Nick Culkin currently holds the record for the shortest ever Premier League debut in history. He set it in

stoppage time in 1999 at Highbury against Arsenal when starting goalie Raimond van der Gouw was injured. In his one and only league appearance after joining Man United from York City four years earlier, Culkin took a free kick and heard the final whistle blow at the same time. He was also the first player to play for Manchester United and non-league side FC United of Manchester.

7. When Alex Stepney joined Man United in 1966 from Chelsea, it was for a fee of £55,000, which was a record at the time. Stepney went on to appear in a goaltending-record 539 outings with the team and helped them win the league title in 1967, enabling them to qualify for the 1968 European Cup. Stepney then backstopped the squad to the famous 4-1 win over Benfica with a memorable save against Eusébio late in the game, which resulted in Eusébio applauding the Englishman.

8. Harry Moger joined the club in May 1903, shortly after it was renamed Manchester United and while they were playing in the Second Division. Many fans didn't believe he had what it took to succeed, but Moger soon established himself as a fine keeper and helped the squad earn promotion to the First Division. He made 264 appearances for the team until 1912 and helped it capture league titles in 1907-08 and 1910-11, as well as the 1909 FA Cup.

9. Harry Gregg of Northern Ireland was considered a hero of the Munich air disaster of 1958 because he helped pull several of his teammates from the burning wreckage after

the crash. He was also a fine goalkeeper. He was voted the best goalkeeper of the 1958 World Cup in Sweden as he helped his nation reach the quarterfinals. Gregg played 247 times for Man United but didn't earn any medals as he was injured for the 1963 FA Cup triumph and didn't play enough games for a medal in 1964-65 and 1966-67 when the team won league crowns.

10. Former English international Gary Bailey grew up in South Africa and was the son of former Ipswich Town keeper Roy Bailey. He made his Man United debut in November 1978 against Ipswich and went on to play 294 league matches until retiring in 1987 due to a serious knee injury. Bailey helped United win the FA Cup in both 1983 and 1985. He became a keynote speaker, author, and TV presenter after hanging up his boots.

CHAPTER 6:

MAESTROS OF THE MIDFIELD

QUIZ TIME!

1. Which legendary midfielder scored 114 goals in league competition with the club?

    a. Ryan Giggs
    b. David Beckham
    c. Bryan Robson
    d. Paul Scholes

2. How many assists did Lee Sharpe have in the 1992-93 Premier League?

    a. 8
    b. 5
    c. 7
    d. 6

3. Paul Ince scored 28 goals with Man United in 281 league matches.

    a. True
    b. False

4. In the 2008 Champions League Final, who replaced Wes Brown and scored the match-winner in a penalty shootout?

   a. Park Ji-sung
   b. Anderson
   c. Owen Hargreaves
   d. Michael Carrick

5. Which midfielder scored seven domestic league goals in 1961-62?

   a. Jimmy Nicholson
   b. Maurice Setters
   c. Nobby Stiles
   d. Warren Bradley

6. Who took 10 penalty kicks in the 2018-19 Premier League?

   a. Paul Pogba
   b. Ander Herrera
   c. Marouane Fellaini
   d. Fred

7. How many appearances did Bryan Robson make in domestic league matches?

   a. 335
   b. 449
   c. 465
   d. 345

8. In 2010-11, 12 different midfielders made at least one appearance in Premier League matches.

   a. True
   b. False

9. Which midfielder received the most yellow cards for the club in the 2005-06 Premier League?

   a. Liam Miller
   b. Darren Fletcher
   c. Roy Keane
   d. José Kléberson

10. Which midfielder recorded 22 assists in all competitive matches in 1999-2000?

   a. Paul Scholes
   b. David Beckham
   c. Jonathan Greening
   d. Quinton Fortune

11. Cristiano Ronaldo was a dedicated left-midfielder when he debuted for Man United in 2003-04.

   a. True
   b. False

12. How many games did Owen Hargreaves play in his four seasons with the club in all competitions?

   a. 36
   b. 27
   c. 23
   d. 14

13. Who appeared in 31 league matches in 2016-17?

   a. Paul Pogba
   b. Matty Willock
   c. Ander Herrera
   d. Angel Gomes

14. Paul Scholes has the most goals of any midfielder in club history as of 2020.

    a. True
    b. False

15. Which player had the most starts of any midfielder in the 2017-18 Premier League season?

    a. Ander Herrera
    b. Daley Blind
    c. Nemanja Matić
    d. Scott McTominay

16. Which midfielder recorded seven assists in the 2019-20 Premier League?

    a. Jesse Lingard
    b. James Garner
    c. Nemanja Matić
    d. Bruno Fernandes

17. Who had eight yellow cards to go along with his eight goals in the 2001-02 Premier League?

    a. Paul Scholes
    b. David Beckham
    c. Juan Sebastián Verón
    d. Michael Stewart

18. In 2015-16, this midfielder played 1,202 minutes in the Premier League.

    a. Bastian Schweinsteiger
    b. Morgan Schneiderlin

c. Memphis Depay

d. Juan Mata

19. Which midfielder scored 13 domestic league goals in 1974-75?

a. Steve Coppell

b. Gerry Daly

c. Sammy McIlroy

d. Jim McCalliog

20. Michael Carrick once earned 35 assists with Man United in a span of 38 league matches.

a. True

b. False

QUIZ ANSWERS

1. A – Ryan Giggs

2. D – 6

3. B – False

4. B – Anderson

5. C – Nobby Stiles

6. A – Paul Pogba

7. D – 345

8. B – False

9. C – Roy Keane

10. B – David Beckham

11. B – False

12. A – 36

13. C – Ander Herrera

14. B – False

15. C – Nemanja Matić

16. D – Bruno Fernandes

17. A – Paul Scholes

18. A – Bastian Schweinsteiger

19. B – Gerry Daly

20. B – False

DID YOU KNOW?

1. Sir Bobby Charlton is a Man United and England legend who had a rocket of a shot with both feet and finished his days with the squad with 249 goals in 758 appearances. The gifted Charlton helped the team win the European Cup in 1968 with two goals while captaining the squad. He won the Ballon d'Or Award for his play two years earlier as well as the World Cup with England. Charlton starred for Man United between 1956 and 1973 and received just two yellow cards during his pro career. He's currently the second-highest scorer for Man United and England (49) behind Wayne Rooney.

2. Some fans may need reminding that former Welsh international midfielder Robbie Savage started out with Man United. The controversial television pundit and reality star couldn't quite make the grade while at Old Trafford as a youth, though, and left the team in 1994. He went on to play with sides such as Crewe Alexandra, Leicester City, Birmingham City, Blackburn Rovers, Derby County, and Brighton & Hove Albion, and played 39 times with Wales.

3. Nicky Butt played with Man United from 1992 to 2004, making 387 appearances, and also played 39 times for England. He returned to Old Trafford in 2012 to help coach the reserve team and was appointed head coach of the youth academy four years later. Butt served as

assistant manager to Ryan Giggs in 2014 when manager David Moyes was fired, and, as a player, he helped the team win six Premier League titles, three FA Cups, a UEFA Champions League, and an Intercontinental Cup.

4. Paul Scholes was regarded as a brilliant play-making and scoring midfielder. The former English international played 66 times for his country and helped Ryan Giggs when Giggs was named interim manager of Man United in 2014. His pro football career lasted from 1993 to 2013, and all 718 of his club games were with United. Scholes originally retired in 2011 but rejoined the squad for a final campaign in 2012-13. He notched 155 goals for United and 14 for England.

5. David Beckham was one of the most famous players in the world during and after his Man United career. He could do it all as a midfielder with his sublime skills, resulting in numerous team and individual titles and awards. He made his first team as a 17-year-old in 1992 and won six Premier League titles, two FA Cups, and a UEFA Champions League crown with the team. Beckham registered 85 goals in 394 outings with the club and scored 17 in 115 contests with England. The term and movie *Bend It Like Beckham* were a tribute to his remarkable free-kick skills.

6. Although once the team's interim manager in 2014, Ryan Giggs is definitely best known for his on-field exploits. He made 963 appearances with the team between 1991 and 2014 after playing at Manchester City as a youth. He has won the most medals in English football history and

played over 1,000 games in all competitions, including 64 for Wales and 4 for Great Britain at the 2012 Olympics in London. Giggs found the back of the net 168 times for United and 12 times for Wales.

7. One member of Man United's famous treble-winning side of 1998-99 was Jonathan Greening. However, he appeared in just 27 games in all competitions for the team after being acquired from York City in 1998. The attacking midfielder didn't earn a cap for England even though he played with the Under-21 squad. To his credit, Greening said he didn't feel that comfortable with receiving a Champions League medal as he didn't set foot on the pitch during the tournament.

8. Northern Ireland international bad boy George Best was known as an international playboy during the Swinging Sixties, and he also owned some of the most exceptional dribbling skills ever witnessed on a football pitch. Best starred with the squad from 1963 to 1974 and tallied 179 goals in 470 outings with Man United and 9 in 37 matches internationally. He finished his pro career with 251 goals in 705 club contests, won the 1968 European Cup with United as well as two league titles, and was named Europe's Player of the Year for 1967-68 when he scored 32 times.

9. Former Scottish international Pat Crerand played for Man United between 1963 and 1971 and won league championships with the club in 1964-65 and 1966-67. He also won the FA Cup in 1962-63 and the European Cup in

1967-68. Crerand played well over 300 games with the side and chipped in with 19 goals. He was a fine holding midfielder, stabilizing force, and solid tackler whose accurate passing skills set up dozens of goals for the likes of George Best, Denis Law, and Bobby Charlton.

10. Starring in the Man United midfield from 1989 to 1995 was Paul Ince, who scored 28 goals in 281 games with the outfit. He was a fine tackler and distributor of the ball and helped the side win two Premier League titles, two FA Cups, a League Cup, a European Cup Winners' Cup, and a European Super Cup. Ince became the first black player to captain England and is also the father of pro player Tom Ince. He didn't see eye to eye with manager Sir Alex Ferguson and was sold to Inter Milan in June 1995.

CHAPTER 7:

SENSATIONAL STRIKERS/FORWARDS

QUIZ TIME!

1. How many Premier League goals did Wayne Rooney score in his first season with Man United?

    a. 5
    b. 11
    c. 8
    d. 10

2. Who scored three penalty kick goals in the 2012-13 Premier League?

    a. Danny Welbeck
    b. Shinji Kagawa
    c. Robin van Persie
    d. Javier Hernández

3. Henrikh Mkhitaryan scored 13 goals and 10 assists in all competitions during his two seasons with the club.

    a. True
    b. False

4. Which forward tallied 121 goals in 275 matches across all competitions for the team?

    a. Ole Gunnar Solskjær
    b. Dwight Yorke
    c. Andy Cole
    d. Eric Cantona

5. Which player scored a brace against Barcelona to win the 1991 UEFA Cup Winners' Cup?

    a. Brian McClair
    b. Mark Robins
    c. Danny Wallace
    d. Mark Hughes

6. How many goals did Tommy Taylor contribute in his 191 appearances?

    a. 120
    b. 131
    c. 117
    d. 106

7. Which forward totaled 20 goals in the 2003-04 Premier League?

    a. Louis Saha
    b. David Bellion
    c. Cristiano Ronaldo
    d. Ruud van Nistelrooy

8. Strikers Jack Rowley and Stan Pearson combined for 52 goals in the 1951-52 league.

a. True

b. False

9. How many goals did Dennis Viollet score against Anderlecht in the second leg of the 1956-57 European Cup?

    a. 4

    b. 1

    c. 3

    d. 2

10. Which striker scored 52 goals in 98 games?

    a. Mark Pearson

    b. Johnny Morris

    c. Billy Whelan

    d. Alex Dawson

11. Ole Gunnar Solskjær earned 55 assists in all competitions during his time with Man United.

    a. True

    b. False

12. How many of Eric Cantona's 82 goals were scored in non-Premier League matches?

    a. 13

    b. 20

    c. 10

    d. 16

13. Which forward tallied 14 assists in Premier League action in 2010-11?

a. Nani

b. Wayne Rooney

c. Dimitar Berbatov

d. Javier Hernández

14. Joe Cassidy scored 90 league goals for Newton Heath, becoming the club's first star player.

a. True

b. False

15. Who scored twice to secure Man United's win in the 1963 FA Cup Final?

a. Bobby Charlton

b. Albert Quixall

c. David Herd

d. Denis Law

16. This forward notched 168 goals in 510 appearances in all competitions with the club between 1919 and 1933.

a. Teddy Partridge

b. Joe Spence

c. Arthur Lochhead

d. Harold Halse

17. Jack Rowley scored how many goals in all competitions in 1947-48?

a. 16

b. 30

c. 10

d. 28

18. Which of these attackers did NOT score 10 or more goals in all competitions in 2018-19?

   a. Anthony Martial
   b. Marcus Rashford
   c. Mason Greenwood
   d. Romelu Lukaku

19. How many goals did Robin van Persie score in 27 Premier League outings in 2015-16?

   a. 12
   b. 18
   c. 13
   d. 10

20. Wayne Rooney scored a Champions League hat trick in his Man United debut.

   a. True
   b. False

QUIZ ANSWERS

1. B – 11

2. C – Robin van Persie

3. A – True

4. C – Andy Cole

5. D – Mark Hughes

6. B – 131

7. D – Ruud van Nistelrooy

8. A – True

9. A – 4

10. C – Billy Whelan

11. B – False

12. D – 16

13. A – Nani

14. A – True

15. C – David Herd

16. B – Joe Spence

17. D – 28

18. C – Mason Greenwood

19. D – 10

20. A – True

DID YOU KNOW?

1. When Portuguese star Cristiano Ronaldo played with Man United, he won several individual honors and also helped the team win three Premier League titles, an FA Cup, two League Cups, the UEFA Champions League, and a FIFA Club World Cup. He also won the Golden Boot in 2007-08 with 31 goals, and he tallied 42 in all competitions. Arguably the greatest player and scorer in history, Ronaldo played with the team from 2003 to 2009 and posted 118 goals in 292 appearances. After the 2019-20 season, Ronaldo had 638 goals in 852 career club games and another 99 in 164 internationals.

2. Colombian international striker Radamel Falcao was considered a bust while at Man United on loan from Monaco for £6 million in 2014-15. He managed just four goals and five assists during his 29 appearances, and the club understandably turned down the option to sign him permanently. His poor play was puzzling considering he had scored 187 goals in 289 games previously while with River Plate, Porto, and Atletico Madrid.

3. At times, Bulgarian international striker Dimitar Berbatov didn't play to his potential at Old Trafford, but that wasn't the case in 2010-11. He helped the squad capture the Premier League and reach the fifth round of the League Cup, the final four of the FA Cup, and the Champions

League Final. Berbatov shared the Golden Boot with Manchester City's Carlos Tevez with 20 goals and was named to the Premier League Team of the Year for a second time. He was also named Bulgarian Player of the Year for a record seventh time.

4. Dutch international Robin van Persie also had an impressive campaign for Man United when he arrived in 2012-13. He made the Premier League Team of the Year for the second consecutive season after winning the Golden Boot with 26 goals. He had won the award the year before with 30 goals for Arsenal. His contributions helped Man United win its 20th top-flight league championship with all three goals in a 3-0 win over Aston Villa to clinch the crown.

5. The often underrated Dwight Yorke of Trinidad and Tobago had an exceptional season for Man United in 1998-99, when they won the treble by taking the Premier League, FA Cup, and Champions League. Yorke led the offense with 29 goals in all competitions, and his 18 league goals saw him share the Golden Boot with Jimmy Floyd Hasselbaink and Michael Owen. Yorke's eight goals also tied for the Champions League scoring lead with Andriy Shevchenko. Yorke made the Premier League Team of the Year and was named the league's Player of the Year.

6. Wayne Rooney is currently the leading scorer of both the English National Team and Man United. He left Old Trafford with 253 goals in 559 outings after breaking the 44-year-old record of 249 goals that Bobby Charlton

achieved in 758 appearances. Rooney scored at a rate of .45 goals per game, with 183 of them coming in the Premier League. He also notched 53 goals in 119 matches with England to break Charlton's mark of 49 in 106 games.

7. Outspoken Eric Cantona played with Man United from 1992 to 1997 and became the club's first captain. He helped the team win five Premier League crowns as well as two League and FA Cup doubles. The French international was known for his technical skill, tenacity, creativity, and scoring ability. Known as "King Eric," he scored 82 goals in 185 games with the team and had 20 goals in 45 outings for France. After retiring, Cantona became involved with beach soccer and making movies.

8. Zlatan Ibrahimović's stint at Old Trafford may have been short, but it was sweet. The Swedish international joined the club in 2016 on a free transfer from Paris Saint-Germain and helped the side win the League Cup and UEFA Europa League during his first campaign. He posted 29 goals for the squad in 53 appearances and is Sweden's all-time international leading scorer with 62 goals in 116 matches.

9. Two of the most important and famous goals scored by Man United came courtesy of Teddy Sheringham and Ole Gunnar Solskjær in stoppage time of the 2-1 UEFA Champions League win over Bayern Munich in 1999. Sheringham arrived in 1997 and won three Premier League titles, an FA Cup, a UEFA Champions League, and an Intercontinental Cup before leaving in 2001. He scored the

equalizer against Bayern and set up for the winner seconds later. He scored 46 goals for the club and another 11 for England.

10. Norman Whiteside of Northern Ireland signed at the age of 17 in 1982 and contributed 68 goals in 278 contests for Man United before being sold to Everton in July 1989. With Manchester, he won a pair of FA Cups and appeared in the 1982 FA Youth Cup Final and 1983 League Cup Final. Whiteside retired at just 26 years old due to a serious knee injury. He set the record for being the youngest player in a World Cup, the youngest to score in a League Cup and FA Cup Final, and the youngest to score a senior goal for Man United.

CHAPTER 8:

NOTABLE TRANSFERS/SIGNINGS

QUIZ TIME!

1. Who was the first player Newton Heath paid a transfer fee for in 1900?

    a. John Grundy

    b. James Fisher

    c. Gilbert Godsmark

    d. Bob Parkinson

2. How much did Newton Heath pay for its first transfer?

    a. £25

    b. £40

    c. £50

    d. £100

3. Manchester United signed Javier Hernández for £7.3 million in 2010.

    a. True

    b. False

4. Which goalkeeper did the club reportedly pay a £2 million transfer fee for in 2005?

    a. Edwin van der Sar
    b. Tim Howard
    c. Ben Foster
    d. Tomasz Kuszczak

5. What was the transfer fee Man United paid S.S. Lazio to acquire Juan Sebastián Verón?

    a. £30 million
    b. £27.5 million
    c. £28.9 million
    d. £29.1 million

6. As of 2020, which player has the club paid the largest fee to acquire?

    a. Paul Pogba
    b. Romelu Lukaku
    c. Rio Ferdinand
    d. Juan Mata

7. Man United sold which player for its highest received transfer fee as of 2020?

    a. Ángel Di María
    b. David Beckham
    c. Cristiano Ronaldo
    d. Romelu Lukaku

8. In April 1900, Man United sold William Bryant to Blackburn Rovers for a fee of £50.

a. True

b. False

9. What club did Man United sign Cristiano Ronaldo from in 2003?

    a. Boavista F.C.

    b. Rio Ave

    c. Sporting CP

    d. Benfica

10. Which player did Man United sell to Ajax for £14 million in 2018?

    a. Marouane Fellaini

    b. Ro-Shaun Williams

    c. Memphis Depay

    d. Daley Blind

11. In 2003, Man United sold David Beckham to Preston North End.

    a. True

    b. False

12. Who was the last player Alex Ferguson signed as club manager in 2012-13?

    a. Ángelo Henríquez

    b. Wilfried Zaha

    c. Shinji Kagawa

    d. Nick Powell

13. Which goalkeeper did the club NOT sign in 1999-2000?

    a. Mark Bosnich

    b. Fabien Barthez

    c. Russel Best

    d. Massimo Taibi

14. In 2016, the team signed Zlatan Ibrahimović on a free transfer.

    a. True

    b. False

15. How much did the club spend to acquire defender Nemanja Vidić?

    a. £8 million

    b. £7 million

    c. £6.5 million

    d. £7.25 million

16. Which player did the club bring in for £30.75 million in 2008-09?

    a. Ritchie De Laet

    b. Zoran Tošić

    c. Fábio

    d. Dimitar Berbatov

17. What club did Man United acquire Denis Irwin from in 1990?

    a. Fulham

    b. Wolverhampton Wanderers

    c. Leeds United

    d. Oldham Athletic

18. What player did Man United sell to S.S. Lazio for £16.5 million in 2001-02?

    a. Jonathan Greening
    b. Andy Cole
    c. Mark Wilson
    d. Jaap Stam

19. For how much did the club sell Phil Neville to Everton in 2005-06?

    a. £3 million
    b. £4 million
    c. £2.5 million
    d. £3.25 million

20. Man United paid £4 million to acquire goalkeeper Massimo Taibi.

    a. True
    b. False

QUIZ ANSWERS

1. C – Gilbert Godsmark

2. B – £40

3. B – False

4. A – Edwin van der Sar

5. D – £29.1 million

6. A – Paul Pogba

7. C – Cristiano Ronaldo

8. A – True

9. C – Sporting CP

10. D – Daley Blind

11. B – False

12. B – Wilfried Zaha

13. C – Russel Best

14. A – True

15. B – £7 million

16. D – Dimitar Berbatov

17. D – Oldham Athletic

18. D – Jaap Stam

19. A – £3 million

20. B – False

DID YOU KNOW?

1. Argentine international defender Gabriel Heinze arrived in Manchester in June 2004 from Paris Saint-Germain for £6.9 million and generally underperformed. He eventually lost his starting position to Patrice Evra and wanted to move to Liverpool in 2007. Manager Sir Alex Ferguson obviously wasn't about to sell him to the team's fiercest rivals, and the saga dragged on. The affair went to a tribunal board that decided Ferguson didn't have to allow Heinze to join Liverpool, and he was sent packing to Real Madrid instead.

2. Man United bought Cristiano Ronaldo from Sporting Lisbon as an 18-year-old in 2003 for €17.5 million. He chipped in with 118 goals and 65 assists in 292 outings and was then sold to Real Madrid for a then world-record €94 million in July 2009, when his market value was rated at €60 million. He went on to become captain of Portugal and one of the planet's best-ever footballers.

3. When the club bought 18-year-old Wayne Rooney from Everton for £25.6 million in 1994, he was the most expensive teenager in history. The money was well spent since Rooney became the all-time leading scorer for Man United and England. Rooney was allowed to leave in July 2009 when he returned to Everton on a free transfer. He then joined D.C. United of MLS in America in June 2018,

and on August 6, 2019, he returned to England as a player/coach with Derby County.

4. Man United paid more for another teenager in June 2014 when they spent £30 million for 18-year-old Luke Shaw of Southampton, which was then a world record for a teenage player. The English international's market value at the time was rated at about a third of what United paid for him. At the conclusion of the 2019-20 season, Shaw had made 139 appearances with the club and helped it win the UEFA Europa League in 2016-17. He was named the team's Sir Matt Busby Player of the Year and the Manchester United Players' Player of the Year for 2018-19.

5. The relationship between Man United and French international midfielder Paul Pogba has been an odd one. Pogba joined the club in 2009 from French team Le Havre in a controversial move and played just seven times before being allowed to leave for Juventus on a free transfer in 2012. Manager Sir Alex Ferguson claimed Pogba disrespected Man United at the time, but in August 2016, the team paid a then world-record £89.3 million to get him back from Juventus.

6. Even Sir Alex Ferguson made a few transfer blunders with Man United. One of them was acquiring Portuguese forward Tiago Manuel Dias Correia, who was commonly known as Bebé. Ferguson reportedly shelled out £7.5 million for Vitória de Guimarães in 2010, even though he'd never seen him play. Ferguson's assistant Carlos Queiroz

recommended the player, but Bebé appeared in only seven matches before being sent out on loan.

7. Argentine international striker Carlos Tevez joined Man United in August 2007, technically on loan from West Ham United. But since third-party ownership was involved with his contract, it was a complicated affair. In July 2009, Tevez signed with Manchester City for a reported British transfer record of £47 million. He was insulted by Man United's contract offer and displeased with his lack of playing time, and many believed he signed with Man City out of spite.

8. Eric Djemba-Djemba was another curious club signing when Sir Alex Ferguson brought the Cameroonian midfielder from Nantes in 2003 to replace former captain Roy Keane. Djemba-Djemba cost just £3.5 million but appeared in only 20 league contests in 18 months before the club sold him to Aston Villa for £1.5 million in 2007. The player then left Aston Villa in 2007 after appearing in just 11 matches and played for numerous other clubs in Scotland, Denmark, Israel, Qatar, Serbia, India, France, Switzerland, and Indonesia before hanging up his boots. Djemba-Djemba reportedly was declared bankrupt after moving to Aston Villa.

9. Former English international midfielder Owen Hargreaves was a fine player when healthy. However, he rarely was. He played with Bayern Munich between 1999 and 2008 with his continuous injury problems culminating in a broken leg in 2006-07. Despite the injury, Man United paid £17 million for Hargreaves. He was with the club four

years and appeared in just 27 league games while making dozens of appearances in the infirmary. Man United released him, and Hargreaves signed with Manchester City for 2011-12 where, unsurprisingly, he made just four appearances.

10. Attacker Ángel Di María was an Argentine international who won the UEFA Champions League with Real Madrid in 2013-14. Man United gobbled him up a few weeks later for a then-British record £59.7 million, and he was given the famous number 7 shirt. He managed just four goals in 32 appearances, though, and then refused to join the club on a 2015 summer tour of America. Di María was promptly sold to Paris Saint-Germain for a fee believed to be between £44 and £48.7 million.

CHAPTER 9:

ODDS & ENDS

QUIZ TIME!

1. How many league matches did Man United win in 1907-08?

    a. 28

    b. 17

    c. 23

    d. 15

2. In 1949-50, the club lost how many domestic league games?

    a. 9

    b. 13

    c. 10

    d. 11

3. Newton Heath originally spent four years in the Alliance Football League.

    a. True

    b. False

4. As of 2020, in how many seasons has the club won exactly 28 games during league play?

   a. 7

   b. 3

   c. 5

   d. 8

5. Which player was nicknamed "the Baby-faced Assassin"?

   a. Ole Gunnar Solskjær

   b. Mark Hughes

   c. Phil Neville

   d. Michael Carrick

6. Of his 345 matches played with the club, how many did David Beckham start for Man United?

   a. 325

   b. 313

   c. 330

   d. 337

7. How many league outings did the club play in 1939-40 before the start of World War II?

   a. 5

   b. 1

   c. 4

   d. 3

8. Fifteen players scored at least one goal across all competitions in 1983-84.

   a. True

   b. False

9. What was Mark Hughes's nickname?

   a. Sparky

   b. Bolts

   c. The Thunder

   d. Shocker

10. The club is commonly referred to by which nickname?

   a. The Demons

   b. The Red Devils

   c. The Reds

   d. The Red and Yellow

11. In 1977-78, Man United won and lost 16 league matches.

   a. True

   b. False

12. Who played the most minutes in the 2007-08 Premier League?

   a. Patrice Evra

   b. Cristiano Ronaldo

   c. Rio Ferdinand

   d. Wes Brown

13. How many Man United players received at least one yellow card in the 1992-93 Premier League?

   a. 11

   b. 8

   c. 12

   d. 5

14. The first time the club was relegated to the Second Division was in 1895-96.

    a. True
    b. False

15. How many goals did the squad score in the 1956-57 league campaign?

    a. 102
    b. 83
    c. 85
    d. 103

16. Which player committed 65 fouls across all competitions in 2015-16?

    a. Wayne Rooney
    b. Anthony Martial
    c. Morgan Schneiderlin
    d. Chris Smalling

17. What is the most goals the club has conceded in one season of league play, as of 2020?

    a. 115
    b. 88
    c. 112
    d. 92

18. What is the nickname of the rivalry between Man United and Manchester City?

    a. The Pennies Derby
    b. North West Derby

c. The Roses Rivalry

d. Manchester Derby

19. Which player had a pass completion of 88.7% (with more than 1,000 passes completed) in all 2019-20 competitions?

a. Nemanja Matić

b. Harry Maguire

c. Victor Lindelöf

d. Paul Pogba

20. Manchester United drew 18 games in the 1980-81 season for a club record, as of 2020.

a. True

b. False

QUIZ ANSWERS

1. C – 23

2. D – 11

3. B – False

4. A – 7

5. A – Ole Gunnar Solskjær

6. B – 313

7. D – 3

8. A – True

9. A – Sparky

10. B – The Red Devils

11. A – True

12. C – Rio Ferdinand

13. A – 11

14. B – False

15. D – 103

16. C – Morgan Schneiderlin

17. A – 115

18. D – Manchester Derby

19. A – Nemanja Matić

20. A – True

DID YOU KNOW?

1. The Manchester Derby between Man United and Man City cooled off in the past when City sometimes played in a lower division. However, the rivalry has been renewed with vigor over the past several years, with both clubs often challenging for the same domestic and European silverware. The sides first battled in 1881 and, as of August 2020, had squared off 182 times in all competitions. United had the edge with 76 wins, 54 defeats, and 52 draws.

2. Man United's fiercest rival is Liverpool. Their rivalry, known as the North West Derby, began in 1894. This is generally regarded as the most famous fixture in England, and it features the nation's two most successful clubs. They have captured numerous domestic, European, and world-based trophies between them, with Man United winning 20 league titles and Liverpool 19. Liverpool has won six European championships to United's three, while United has won 66 trophies and Liverpool 64. United also has the edge in derby meetings, as of August 2020, with 80 wins, 67 losses, and 57 draws.

3. Man United hosted Arsenal in a First Division match in October 1990, and the 1-0 Arsenal victory erupted into a brawl. Twenty-one of the 22 players were involved, although it lasted no more than a minute, and just two players were booked. However, both clubs fined several of

their players. A month later, both teams were fined £50,000, while Arsenal had two league points deducted and Man United one point. This incident started an intense rivalry between the sides.

4. During a January 1995 Premier League game at Selhurst Park between Man United and Crystal Palace, United's Eric Cantona was sent off with a red card in the second half. As he was making his way to the tunnel, a fan hurled verbal abuse at him, which led to the Frenchman flying feet first into the crowd to deliver a well-aimed kung fu kick to the perpetrator. Cantona received an eight-month ban and was fined heavily by the club for his actions. To make matters worse, Blackburn went on to win the league that season.

5. Sadly, Duncan Edwards passed away at the age of 21 due to injuries suffered in the 1958 Munich air disaster. The English international midfielder played 177 times for Man United and 18 times for his country and was one of the famous "Busby Babes." Edwards signed with the club as a teenager and became the youngest player ever to appear in the First Division and the youngest to represent England since World War II. He helped United secure two league championships and reach the European Cup semifinals before his death.

6. Alan Smith is certainly a common name in Britain; two of them have played for England. One of the Alan Smiths played with Man United. The tough forward/midfielder made a name for himself with Leeds United from 1998 to

2004, when he joined Man United for £7 million. Smith suffered several injuries. The worst was in February 2006, when he dislocated his ankle and broke his leg in an FA Cup match in Liverpool. He was sold to Newcastle for approximately £6 million in 2007 and left Old Trafford with 93 appearances and 12 goals to his name.

7. As of August 2020, over 925 players have played for Man United since the club's first competitive match, but only 10 have appeared in 500 games or more. They are Ryan Giggs (963), Bobby Charlton (758), Paul Scholes (718), Bill Foulkes (688), Gary Neville (602), Wayne Rooney (559), Alex Stepney (539), Tony Dunne (535), Denis Irwin (529), and Joe Spence (510).

8. The Man United club crest is based on the Manchester City Council coat of arms; however, the current crest retains only a ship in full sail. The devil comes from the nickname "the Red Devils" and was included in the crest in 1970. The crest was added to the jersey a year later. Newton Heath's uniform included green and gold jerseys between 1894 and 1896, when they were changed to white shirts and navy blue shorts. When Manchester United was born in 1902, the colors were changed to red shirts with white shorts and black socks.

9. The Manchester United Women Football Club was founded in May 2018 and is based in Broughton, Greater Manchester, which is approximately 1.5 miles from Manchester city center. The professional outfit competes in England's Women's Super League (WSL), which is the top

tier of women's football in the country after being promoted from the championship at the conclusion of 2018-19. The team currently plays its home games at Leigh Sports Village and is also nicknamed the Red Devils.

10. In 2016-17, Man United was ranked as the world's highest-earning football club with annual revenue of €676.3 million. The club was rated as the third most valuable club in the world in 2019, when it was valued at £3.15 billion ($3.81 billion). In 2015, Man United was ranked as the most valuable football brand on the planet at $1.2 billion.

CHAPTER 10:

DOMESTIC COMPETITION

QUIZ TIME!

1. How many top-flight league titles has Man United won as of 2020?

    a. 18
    b. 19
    c. 20
    d. 21

2. Which team did the club defeat to win its first FA Cup in 1909?

    a. Norwich City
    b. Everton
    c. Newcastle United
    d. Bristol City

3. The club's longest streak without winning a league title is 48 years.

    a. True
    b. False

4. What year did the club win its first league title in the Premier League?

   a. 1995-96
   b. 2005-06
   c. 1992-93
   d. 2008-09

5. How many Community Shields has Man United won or shared as of 2020?

   a. 21
   b. 17
   c. 15
   d. 22

6. Manchester had how many points to win its first league title in 1907-08?

   a. 42
   b. 37
   c. 52
   d. 62

7. How many League Cups has Man United won as of 2020?

   a. 5
   b. 3
   c. 4
   d. 6

8. Manchester United completed its first domestic league treble in 1993-94.

   a. True
   b. False

9. How many times has Man United shared the Community Shield?

    a. 2
    b. 3
    c. 4
    d. 5

10. What team did the club beat to win its first League (EFL) Cup in 1992?

    a. Nottingham Forest
    b. Middlesbrough
    c. Tottenham Hotspur
    d. Portsmouth

11. The club appeared in the first-ever FA Community Shield match in 1908.

    a. True
    b. False

12. What team did the club defeat to win its first Community Shield?

    a. Northampton Town
    b. Chelsea
    c. Fulham
    d. Queens Park Rangers

13. Which domestic title did the club NOT win in 2008-09?

    a. League Title
    b. FA Cup
    c. Community Shield
    d. EFL Cup

14. The club won eight of its league titles in the Football League First Division.

    a. True

    b. False

15. Man United has won the FA Cup a total of how many times, as of 2020?

    a. 13

    b. 8

    c. 10

    d. 12

16. The club has been a runner-up to which title four times, as of 2020?

    a. League Title

    b. FA Cup

    c. League (EFL) Cup

    d. Community Shield

17. As of 2020, how many times has Man United achieved the double (League Title and FA Cup)?

    a. 3

    b. 5

    c. 2

    d. 4

18. Man United has won the Community Shield outright how many times?

    a. 15

    b. 17

c. 16

d. 14

19. How many times did Man United win the Second Division title?

    a. 1

    b. 3

    c. 0

    d. 2

20. Man United was the first English team to win the FA Cup/League Title double twice.

    a. True

    b. False

QUIZ ANSWERS

1. C – 20

2. D – Bristol City

3. B – False

4. C – 1992-93

5. A – 21

6. C – 52

7. A – 5

8. B – False

9. C – 4

10. A – Nottingham Forest

11. A – True

12. D – Queens Park Rangers

13. B – FA Cup

14. B – False

15. D – 12

16. C – League (EFL) Cup

17. A – 3

18. B – 17

19. D – 2

20. A – True

DID YOU KNOW?

1. Man United has won 20 top-flight league titles throughout club history up to 2020, which is currently an English record. This includes the 13 in the Premier League, which launched in 1992-93, and seven in the former First Division. The squad won crowns in the following campaigns: 1907-08, 1910-11, 1951-52, 1955-56, 1956-57, 1964-65, 1966-67, 1992-93, 1993-94, 1995-96, 1996-97, 1998-99, 1999-2000, 2000-01, 2002-03, 2006-07, 2007-08, 2008-09, 2010-11, and 2012-13. The team also won the Second Division title in 1935-36 and 1974-75.

2. The FA Cup has been won a dozen times by Man United. Its victories came in 1908-09, 1947-48, 1962-63, 1976-77, 1982-83, 1984-85, 1989-90, 1993-94, 1995-96, 1998-99, 2003-04, and 2015-16. In addition, the club won the English League Cup five times, in 1991-92, 2005-06, 2008-09, 2009-10, and 2016-17.

3. The FA Community Shield, formerly the FA Charity Shield, traditionally kicks off the English season with the FA Cup holders playing the winners of the Premier League (former First Division). Man United holds the current record with 17 wins and four shared titles when the game ended in a draw. Its wins came in 1908, 1911, 1952, 1956, 1957, 1983, 1993, 1994, 1996, 1997, 2003, 2007, 2008, 2010, 2011, 2013, and 2016, with draws in 1965, 1967, 1977, and 1990.

4. Man United was humbled at home 3-0 by third-tier (Division Two) side 0-3 York City in the second round of the 1995-96 League Cup, even though its starting lineup featured Phil Neville, Ryan Giggs, Brian McClair, Gary Pallister, Lee Sharpe, Ryan Giggs, Denis Irwin, and Paul Parker. United was down to 10 men in the second half, when Pat McGibbon was sent off in his senior debut for the team, but the performance and result were still shocking. United won the second leg 3-1, but they lost 4-3 on aggregate.

5. Another League Cup meltdown occurred in the second round of the 2014-15 competition in August 2014, when the MK Dons trounced Man United 4-0 at home. Manager Louis van Gaal's squad was bubbling that day as United had just signed Ángel di María from Real Madrid, but third-tier (League One) Milton Keynes showed them no mercy even though David de Gea was in goal and the starting squad included Shinji Kagawa, Javier Hernández, and Danny Welbeck.

6. One of the club's biggest FA Cup upsets came in January 1984, when Third Division Bournemouth hosted First Division Man United in a third-round tie at Dean Court. As Cup holders, United was a huge favorite, but it didn't matter, as Bournemouth was the better side on the pitch, where it mattered. They capitalized on their chances to take a 2-0, and, although United attempted to get back in the game, they couldn't find the back of the net. The Red Devils learned from the humiliation, though, and reclaimed the FA Cup a year later.

7. Norwich City, which was in the Third Division at the time, had knocked Man United out of the FA Cup eight years earlier at home. When the teams met again in the fourth round of the FA Cup in February 1967, revenge was on United's mind against its foes, who were now in the Second Division. Sir Matt Busby had World Cup winners Nobby Stiles and Bobby Charlton in the starting 11, along with Pat Crerand, Denis Law, George Best, and goalkeeper Alex Stepney, but Norwich left Old Trafford with a 2-1 win.

8. Although Man United's haul of 12 FA Cups is second only to Arsenal's current record of 14, the club also co-shares the record of eight defeats in the Final with Everton. United was beaten in the final match in 1957, 1958, 1976, 1979, 1995, 2005, 2007, and 2018. Its 20 appearances in the Final is second only to Arsenal's record of 21.

9. The 1978-79 FA Cup Final between Man United and Arsenal will always be remembered for its dramatic ending. Arsenal led 2-0 at halftime, but United pulled a goal back through Gordon McQueen in the 86th minute. Sammy McIlroy then notched a sensational equalizer just two minutes later, and it looked like the match was headed to extra time. However, Alan Sunderland scored in the final minute to give Arsenal a 3-2 win in what has been dubbed the "Five-Minute Final."

10. The club's biggest FA Cup Final wins were 4-0 over Chelsea in 1993-94 and against Brighton & Hove Albion in 1982-83. The win over Brighton came in a replay on May

26, 1983, at Wembley Stadium, after the clubs had played to a 2-2 draw at the same venue five days earlier. The victory over Chelsea was also held at Wembley on May 14, 1994, and it gave Man United its first-ever double as the club clinched the Premier League by eight points over Blackburn before the Cup Final.

CHAPTER 11:

EUROPE & BEYOND

QUIZ TIME!

1. What was the first European title the club won in 1967-68?

    a. European Super Cup

    b. European Cup

    c. Europa League

    d. Cup Winners' Cup

2. Which team did Man United defeat to win its first European Super Cup?

    a. Ajax

    b. Olympique de Marseille

    c. Barcelona

    d. Red Star Belgrade

3. Manchester United has won a total of 10 European and international championships.

    a. True

    b. False

4. How many times has the club won the UEFA Intercontinental Cup?

    a. 1
    b. 2
    c. 3
    d. 4

5. Which squad did Man United beat to win its first FIFA Club World Cup?

    a. Liga Deportiva Universitaria
    b. Gamba Osaka
    c. Al Ahly SC
    d. C.F. Pachuca

6. What season did the club win its first Europa League title?

    a. 2014-15
    b. 2015-16
    c. 2016-17
    d. 2018-19

7. Man United defeated which Dutch outfit to win its first Europa League title?

    a. Feyenoord Rotterdam
    b. Ajax
    c. FC Twente
    d. SBV Vitesse

8. In 2008-09, Man United competed for three different European trophies.

    a. True
    b. False

9. Which club did Man United face in the 1967-68 European Cup semifinal?

    a. Górnik Zabrze

    b. Sparta Prague

    c. FK Sarajevo

    d. Real Madrid

10. How many times did Man United compete for the Cup Winners' Cup?

    a. 1

    b. 3

    c. 5

    d. 2

11. In the 2007-08 Champions League, Man United defeated Chelsea 6-5 in a penalty shootout.

    a. True

    b. False

12. Which player won Man of the Match for Man United in the 2007-08 Champions League Final?

    a. Rio Ferdinand

    b. Wayne Rooney

    c. Edwin van der Sar

    d. Cristiano Ronaldo

13. Which Brazilian club did Man United defeat to win the UEFA Intercontinental Cup?

    a. Sociedade Esportiva Palmeiras

    b. Sport Club Internacional

c. Santos FC

d. São Paulo FC

14. In 2010-11, Man United was runner-up in the European Super Cup.

   a. True

   b. False

15. How many times has Man United won the European Cup/UEFA Champions League as of 2020?

   a. 5

   b. 2

   c. 4

   d. 3

16. Which side did Man United NOT face in the 1998-99 Champions League group stage?

   a. ŁKS Łódź

   b. Bayern Munich

   c. Brøndby IF

   d. Barcelona

17. What was the final score of Man United's 1991 Cup Winners' Cup Final?

   a. 2-1

   b. 1-0

   c. 2-0

   d. 3-2

18. As of 2020, how many total European trophies have Man United won?

a. 8

b. 5

c. 6

d. 7

19. Man United did NOT play against which club in the 2016-17 Europa League?

    a. Celta de Vigo

    b. Anderlecht

    c. FC Rostov

    d. KRC Genk

20. The club became the first British team to win a treble by winning the 1999 League Title, FA Cup, and Champions League.

    a. True

    b. False

QUIZ ANSWERS

1. B – European Cup

2. D – Red Star Belgrade

3. B – False

4. A – 1

5. A – Liga Deportiva Universitaria

6. C – 2016-17

7. B – Ajax

8. B – False

9. D – Real Madrid

10. C – 5

11. A – True

12. C – Edwin van der Sar

13. A – Sociedade Esportiva Palmeiras

14. B – False

15. D – 3

16. A – ŁKS Łódź

17. A – 2-1

18. C – 6

19. D – KRC Genk

20. A – True

DID YOU KNOW?

1. Man United has been quite successful on the international level, having won several pieces of silverware in Europe and beyond. As of 2020, here is a list of the club's achievements: European Cup/UEFA Champions League (1967-68, 1998-99, 2007-08), European Cup Winners' Cup (1990-91), UEFA Europa League (2016-17), European Super Cup (1991), Intercontinental Cup (1999), and FIFA Club World Cup (2008).

2. The Intercontinental Cup was also referred to as the European/South American Cup and the Toyota Cup and was contested between 1960 and 2004. It was sanctioned by UEFA and CONMEBOL with one finalist from Europe and one from South America, generally the winner of the UEFA Champions League and the South American Copa Libertadores. The competition was then renamed the FIFA Club World Cup. Man United is the only British team to win the silverware, as they beat Palmeiras of Brazil 1-0 in 1999. They were also runners-up in 1968 when they were edged 2-1 over two legs by Estudiantes of Argentina.

3. The FIFA Club World Cup is operated by FIFA, has been in existence since 2000, and has been hosted by several different nations. In 2005, the FIFA Club World Championship merged with the Intercontinental Cup and was renamed the FIFA Club World Cup a year later. The

tournament features winners of various global competitions including the UEFA Champions League holders. Man United became the first British winners in 2008 in Japan with a 1-0 victory over Liga Deportiva Universitaria (Liga de Quito) of Ecuador courtesy of a Wayne Rooney goal in the 73rd minute. Liverpool won it in 2019.

4. The club made history on May 29, 1968, at "home" at Wembley, when Matt Busby's squad downed Benfica 4-1 in extra time in its first appearance in the European Cup Final. They became the second British team, after Glasgow Celtic of Scotland, to be crowned champions of Europe and the first English squad. Bobby Charlton scored in the 53rd minute, but Jaime Graça equalized for Benfica with 11 minutes remaining. George Best scored in the 92nd minute followed by Brian Kidd, on his 19th birthday, just two minutes later with Charlton adding another in the 99th minute.

5. In the 1998-99 UEFA Champions League Final in Barcelona, Bayern Munich led Man United after just six minutes and appeared to be in control. The scene changed, though, when Teddy Sheringham scored 36 seconds into second-half stoppage time to level the contest. Fellow substitute Ole Gunnar Solskjær scored 101 seconds later to complete the dramatic comeback and give Man United its second European crown. The victory meant United was the first English team to win a treble, as they had captured the FA Cup and Premier League earlier that year.

6. The club's third European Championship came in 2007-08

against fellow Premier League side Chelsea in Moscow, Russia. Man United took the title with a 6-5 conquest in a penalty shootout following a 1-1 draw after 90 and 120 minutes. Cristiano Ronaldo headed United in front after 26 minutes with Frank Lampard equalizing for Chelsea just before halftime. Chelsea's Didier Drogba received a red card in the 86th minute, but United couldn't take advantage. Ronaldo missed the team's third shootout penalty, meaning John Terry could win the match, but he hit the post. Keeper Edwin van der Sar then saved Chelsea's seventh shot to seal the victory.

7. Wayne Rooney made his Man United debut as an 18-year-old at home against Fenerbahce of Turkey in the 2004-05 Champions League, and it was a night to remember. Rooney scored in the 17th minute from 20 yards to give United a 2-0 lead and banged one in from 25 yards 11 minutes later to make it 3-0. With his squad up 3-1 in the 54th minute, Rooney curled in a tremendous free kick to complete his hat trick. United was a 6-2 winner, and Rooney made an everlasting impression on the team's supporters.

8. Man United owns the mark for the longest away undefeated streak in the Champions League at 16 games. It began with a 1-0 group stage conquest of Sporting CP in 2007-08 and was halted with a 2-1 loss to Bayern Munich during the first leg of the 2009-10 quarterfinals. United was beaten 2-0 in the 2009 Final by Barcelona, but the match was held at a neutral site and didn't affect the streak.

United also holds the record for the longest undefeated streak at 25 games. It kicked off with the victory over Sporting CP in 2007-08 and ended with the 2-0 defeat to Barcelona in the 2009 Final.

9. The club had a 2-1 aggregate lead on Real Madrid in the 2013 Champions League quarterfinals at home in the second leg with 34 minutes remaining. Portuguese international Nani then caught Real Madrid's Alvaro Arbeloa with an apparent unintentional high kick and received a red card from referee Cüneyt Çakır. The inevitable then happened as Real scored twice against Man United to reach the semifinals. United claimed Nani was simply trying to play the ball, but Çakır insisted it was still a dangerous play. Real manager José Mourinho remarked that his team got a lucky break and didn't really deserve the win.

10. Defensively, Man United holds the current Champions League record for the longest run without allowing a goal from the start of a season. They went 481 minutes without conceding in 2010-11, with their first goal against coming in the 32nd minute of their sixth group stage game. The club is also the only one to play six away matches in a Champions League campaign without allowing a goal, also in 2010-11.

CHAPTER 12:

TOP SCORERS

QUIZ TIME!

1. Joe Cassidy scored an even 100 goals in how many games for the club?

    a. 100

    b. 121

    c. 174

    d. 221

2. Which player tallied 100 goals in 319 total appearances with the team?

    a. Frank Stapleton

    b. Brian Kidd

    c. George Wall

    d. Tommy Reid

3. Javier "Chicharito" Hernández tallied 72 goals in 157 outings with the squad.

    a. True

    b. False

4. Bob Donaldson notched 66 goals for Newton Heath in 155 contests. What was his nationality?

    a. English
    b. Welsh
    c. Northern Irish
    d. Scottish

5. How many Premier League goals did Marcus Rashford contribute in 2019-20?

    a. 15
    b. 12
    c. 17
    d. 31

6. Which forward scored three FA Cup goals in 11 appearances during his Man United career?

    a. Andy Cole
    b. Ruud van Nistelrooy
    c. Dwight Yorke
    d. Joe Spence

7. Which player scored 16 goals for Man United in his 55 games in European competitions?

    a. Cristiano Ronaldo
    b. Ryan Giggs
    c. Paul Scholes
    d. Gary Neville

8. Cristiano Ronaldo tallied 37 league goals in 34 games in 2006-07.

a. True

b. False

9. Lou Macari played how many games to reach the 97-goal mark with the team?

    a. 282

    b. 311

    c. 401

    d. 425

10. Former skipper Bryan Robson scored how many League Cup goals in 51 matches with the side?

    a. 8

    b. 6

    c. 15

    d. 5

11. Enoch West chipped in with 80 goals in 181 outings with the club.

    a. True

    b. False

12. Which forward registered 61 goals in 162 games with the Red Devils?

    a. Stuart Pearson

    b. Robin van Persie

    c. Charlie Mitten

    d. Jack Peddie

13. Who led the club with 26 goals in 2012-13 to win the Premier League Golden Boot?

a. Robin van Persie

b. Nani

c. Danny Welbeck

d. Shinji Kagawa

14. Harold Halse scored 56 times in 125 outings for the club between 1908 and 1912.

a. True

b. False

15. Tommy Bamford, who notched 57 goals in 109 games for Man United, played five internationals for which nation?

a. Canada

b. USA

c. Jamaica

d. Wales

16. Which forward was credited with 56 goals in 184 appearances with Man United?

a. Albert Quixall

b. Dimitar Berbatov

c. Harry Rowley

d. Arthur Lochhead

17. How many goals did Shinji Kagawa tally in 20 Premier League matches in 2012-13?

a. 0

b. 3

c. 6

d. 12

18. The most goals scored by Wayne Rooney in a Premier League season with Man United was?

    a. 21
    b. 26
    c. 27
    d. 31

19. Whose career-high in goals for a season with Man United in all competitions was 16?

    a. Eric Cantona
    b. David Beckham
    c. Sammy McIlroy
    d. Norman Whiteside

20. Dennis Viollet scored an even 20 league goals in both the 1954-55 and 1955-56 campaigns.

    a. True
    b. False

QUIZ ANSWERS

1. C – 174

2. C – George Wall

3. B – False

4. D – Scottish

5. C – 17

6. C – 3

7. A – Cristiano Ronaldo

8. B – False

9. C – 401

10. D – 5

11. A – True

12. C – Charlie Mitten

13. A – Robin van Persie

14. A – True

15. D – Wales

16. A – Albert Quixall

17. C – 6

18. C – 27

19. B – David Beckham

20. A –True

DID YOU KNOW?

1. As of September 2020, the top 20 scorers in all competitions combined in Man United history were Wayne Rooney, 253; Sir Bobby Charlton, 249; Denis Law, 237; Jack Rowley, 211; Dennis Viollet, 179; George Best, 179; Joe Spence, 168; Ryan Giggs, 168; Mark Hughes, 163; Paul Scholes, 155; Ruud van Nistelrooy, 150; Stan Pearson, 148; David Herd 145; Tommy Taylor, 131; Brian McClair, 127; Ole Gunnar Solskjær, 126; Andy Cole, 121; Cristiano Ronaldo, 118; Sandy Turnbull, 101; and George Wall and Joe Cassidy, each with an even 100.

2. Scottish international forward Denis Law signed with Manchester City for a then-British record of £55,000 in 1960. A year later, he joined Torino in Italy for £110,000 and then signed with Man United for £115,000 in 1962 to set another British transfer high. He spent 11 years at Old Trafford, scoring 237 goals in 404 games. In 1964, he became the only Scottish player to win the Ballon d'Or Award. Unfortunately for Law, he missed the 1968 European Cup victory due to injury. He left United in 1973 to play his final season with Man City. Law shares the all-time scoring lead for Scotland with 30 goals in 55 games and holds the Man United record for goals in a season with 46.

3. English international forward John Rowley played 17

years with Man United from 1937 to 1954 and was known by the nickname "The Gunner" due to his explosive shooting and tremendous goal-scoring skills. He left the team to become player/manager of Plymouth Argyle and then remained in management, taking over Ajax of Amsterdam in 1963-64. He helped Man United win the 1947-48 FA Cup and the First Division title in 1951-52. His brother, Arthur Rowley, scored 434 goals in 619 league games to set the record for the most goals ever in English league football.

4. Striker Dennis Viollet joined Man United in 1949 after coming up through the junior ranks and survived the Munich air disaster nine years later. He helped the squad win league titles in 1955-56 and 1956-57 and played in partnership with fellow striker Tommy Taylor. Viollet scored 179 goals in 293 games with United; 4 of them came in a 10-0 rout of Belgian champions Anderlecht in 1956. Viollet set a club record in 1959-60 with 32 goals in 36 contests and soon earned his only two caps for England. Sir Matt Busby sold him to Stoke City in 1962 for £25,000.

5. Tommy Taylor was a natural scorer with 16 goals in 19 matches for England and 131 in 191 appearances with Man United. The center-forward scored 28 goals in 46 outings for Barnsley to attract the attention of Man United where the 21-year-old was transferred to in March 1953 for the odd amount of £29,999. He scored twice in his United debut and helped the team win league titles in 1955-56 and 1956-57. Sir Matt Busby turned down £65,000 for Taylor

from Inter Milan in 1957, and, sadly, the 26-year-old lost his life in the Munich air disaster a year later.

6. Another fine scorer for Man United was Andy Cole, who notched 121 goals in 275 encounters between 1995 and 2001. As of 2020, he was the third-highest scorer ever in the Premier League with 187 goals. Cole won the PFA Young Player of the Year award and Golden Boot during his career as well as five League titles, two FA Cups, and the UEFA Champions League with United. The English international forward was the first to score five goals in a Premier League match, when United thumped Ipswich Town 9-0 in 1995.

7. Mark Hughes may be well known as a manager to younger fans, but he netted 163 goals in 467 games with Man United in two separate stints between 1983-84 and 1994-95. Hughes also played in Europe with Barcelona and Bayern Munich, scored 16 goals in 72 contests for Wales, and was the first player to receive the PFA Players' Player of the Year award twice, in 1989 and 1991. While playing with United, Hughes helped the club win two Premier League crowns, three FA Cups, a League Cup, the European Cup Winners' Cup, and the European Super Cup.

8. In 1919, Joe Spence made his debut with Man United when the league resumed action for the first time after World War I. He played with the club until 1933 and registered 168 goals in 510 appearances, both of which were club records when he left. Spence typically played center-forward or right wing and the terrace chant "Give it

to Joe" was one of the most common at Old Trafford during his time there. Spence scored once in his two appearances with England and returned to the club in 1945 as a coach and scout.

9. Dutch international striker Ruud van Nistelrooy tallied 150 goals in 219 outings with Man United after arriving from PSV Eindhoven in 2001 and before he joined Real Madrid in 2006. He led the scoring in three UEFA Champions League campaigns and notched 56 career goals in the competition. Van Nistelrooy also won Golden Boots in three different European leagues. He joined United for a then-British record £19 million and helped the squad win the Premier League, FA Cup, and League Cup. Twice, he won the Sir Matt Busby Player of the Year award.

10. David Herd made a name for himself with 107 goals in 180 games for Arsenal before joining Man United for £35,000 in 1961. He was at Old Trafford until 1968 and scored another 145 goals in 265 appearances. He helped the team win the 1962-63 FA Cup by scoring twice in the Final. He also helped United win league crowns in 1964-65 and 1966-67 and was a member of the squad that captured the '68 European Cup. Herd once scored a hat trick against three different Sunderland goalkeepers in a 5-0 victory in 1966. He left on a free transfer to Stoke City, scored three times in five games for Scotland, and later managed Lincoln City.

CONCLUSION

At the time, nobody knew Newton Heath would evolve into one of the most phenomenal sporting entities on the planet when the small football club became Manchester United F.C. in 1902.

The story has been written for well over a century now that the "Red Devils" have been thrilling fans across the globe with its exciting brand of football. The sheer number of Man United supporters across the world has resulted in the club becoming one of the richest and most successful in the history of all professional sports.

Even with numerous league championships, FA Cups, League Cups, and European silverware under their belts, Man United has never been more determined than now to add more and more silverware to its trophy case at Old Trafford.

The trivia/fact book you've just read through deals with the club's history from the day it began in 1878 right up until the very last game of the infamous, COVID-19-affected 2019-20 Premier League season.

This book contains a wide range of facts, trivia questions, and anecdotes about your favorite Man United players and managers. The controversial moments, transfer busts, and Cup upsets haven't been left out because history is history whether it's favorable or not.

Our goal was to dig up as much Man United trivia as possible and present it in a lighthearted and fun manner so supporters are given the opportunity to relive all the exciting and disappointing moments the club has served up throughout its legendary history.

We certainly hope it was an enjoyable way to test your loyalty and knowledge of the club and perhaps learn something new at the same time.

With this much trivia and factual information within your grasp, you will find yourself in a perfect position to prepare for the next trivia contest or challenge that comes your way from fellow Man United supporters, friends, and family members.

Man United supporters have proven time and time again that they are among the most vocal and passionate in the history of sports and stand by their club regardless of the outcome. We hope this trivia book will help out the next time you're challenged to a trivia showdown about this historic and legendary football club.

Thanks for standing by the team through thick and thin and taking the time to read through our newest Man United trivia/fact book.

Made in the USA
Las Vegas, NV
10 December 2023

82460727R00075